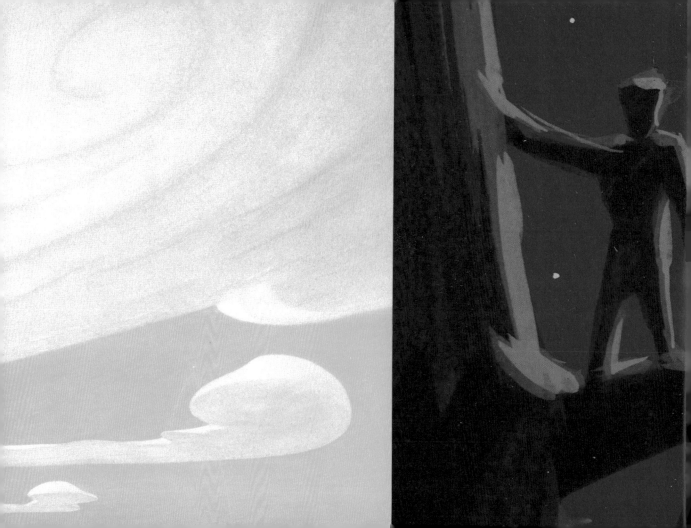

FROM DISNEY'S HERCULES

GO THE DISTANCE

MUSIC BY ALAN MENKEN
LYRICS BY DAVID ZIPPEL

HYPERION

NEW YORK

I HAVE OFTEN DREAMED
OF A FAR OFF PLACE

WHERE A HERO'S WELCOME
WOULD BE WAITING FOR ME

V

WHERE THE CROWDS WILL CHEER
WHEN THEY SEE MY FACE

VI

AND A VOICE KEEPS SAYING
THIS IS WHERE I'M MEANT TO BE

VIII

I'LL BE THERE SOMEDAY
I CAN GO THE DISTANCE

X

I WILL FIND MY WAY
IF I CAN BE STRONG

I KNOW EVR'Y MILE
WILL BE WORTH MY WHILE

WHEN I GO THE DISTANCE
I'LL BE RIGHT WHERE I BELONG

DOWN AN UNKNOWN ROAD
TO EMBRACE MY FATE

THOUGH THAT ROAD MAY WANDER
IT WILL LEAD ME TO YOU

XIX

AND A THOUSAND YEARS
WOULD BE WORTH THE WAIT

IT MAY TAKE A LIFETIME
BUT SOMEHOW I'LL SEE IT THROUGH

XX

AND I WON'T LOOK BACK
I CAN GO THE DISTANCE

XXII

AND I'LL STAY ON TRACK
NO I WON'T ACCEPT DEFEAT

IT'S AN UPHILL SLOPE
BUT I WON'T LOSE HOPE

TILL I GO THE DISTANCE
AND MY JOURNEY IS COMPLETE

BUT TO LOOK BEYOND THE GLORY
IS THE HARDEST PART

FOR A HERO'S STRENGTH IS MEASURED BY HIS HEART

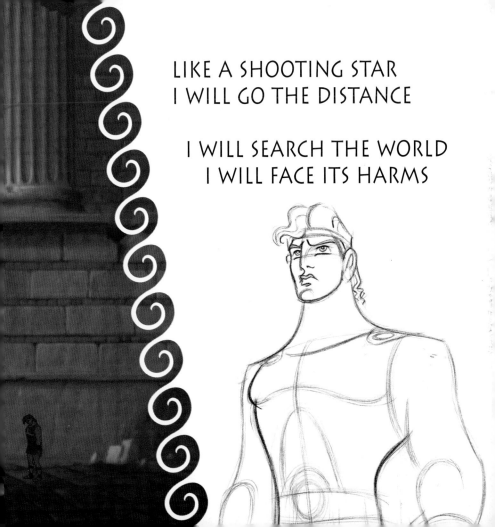

LIKE A SHOOTING STAR
I WILL GO THE DISTANCE

I WILL SEARCH THE WORLD
I WILL FACE ITS HARMS

I DON'T CARE HOW FAR
I CAN GO THE DISTANCE

TILL I FIND MY HERO'S WELCOME
WAITING IN YOUR ARMS

XLIII

I WILL SEARCH THE WORLD
I WILL FACE ITS HARMS

TILL I FIND MY HERO'S WELCOME
WAITING IN YOUR ARMS

XLV

"GO THE DISTANCE"
MUSIC BY ALAN MENKEN
LYRICS BY DAVID ZIPPEL
© 1997 WONDERLAND MUSIC COMPANY, INC.
AND WALT DISNEY MUSIC COMPANY
ALL RIGHTS RESERVED. USED BY PERMISSION.

ADAPTED FROM
WALT DISNEY PICTURES' HERCULES
MUSIC BY ALAN MENKEN LYRICS BY DAVID ZIPPEL ORIGINAL SCORE BY ALAN MENKEN
PRODUCED BY ALICE DEWEY AND JOHN MUSKER & RON CLEMENTS
DIRECTED BY JOHN MUSKER & RON CLEMENTS

FOR INFORMATION ADDRESS:
HYPERION
114 FIFTH AVENUE, NEW YORK, NY 10011

PRODUCED BY:
WELCOME ENTERPRISES, INC.
575 BROADWAY, NEW YORK, NY 10012

DESIGN BY JON GLICK

ISBN 0-7868-6295-5

FIRST EDITION
2 4 6 8 10 9 7 5 3 1
PRINTED IN JAPAN BY TOPPAN PRINTING CO., INC.

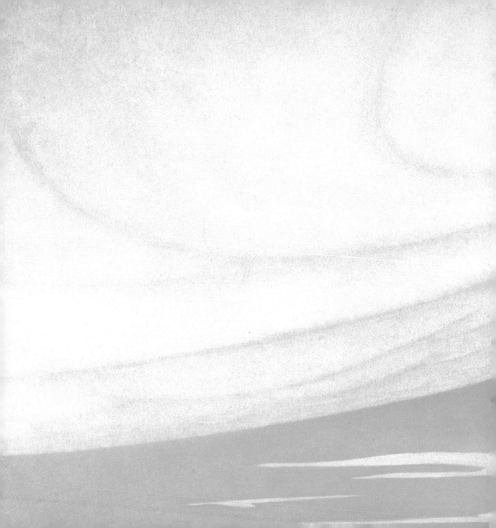